The War Being Waged

The War Being Waged

Darla Contois

SCIROCCO DRAMA

The War Being Waged
first published 2022 by Scirocco Drama
An imprint of J. Gordon Shillingford Publishing Inc.
© 2022 Darla Contois
Scirocco Drama Editor: Glenda MacFarlane
Cover design by Doowah Design
Author photo by Patrick Shannon
Production photos by Joey Senft

Printed and bound in Canada on 100% post-consumer recycled paper.
We acknowledge the financial support of the Manitoba Arts Council and
The Canada Council for the Arts for our publishing program.

Production inquiries to:
ad@pte.mb.ca

Library and Archives Canada Cataloguing in Publication

Title: The war being waged / Darla Contois.
Names: Contois, Darla, author.
Identifiers: Canadiana 20220429804 | ISBN 9781990737183 (softcover)
Subjects: LCGFT: Drama.
Classification: LCC PS8605.O589 W37 2022 | DDC C812/.6,Äîdc23

J. Gordon Shillingford Publishing
P.O. Box 86, RPO Corydon Avenue, Winnipeg, MB Canada R3M 3S3

The War Being Waged *is dedicated to any and all families still experiencing colonization under the Dominion of Canada.*

And, to my mom for all of her love and support of my voice as a writer. I love you.

Darla Contois

Darla Contois is a Cree-Saulteaux performer and playwright. She graduated from the Centre for Indigenous Theatre's professional training program in 2014 and attended David Smukler's National Voice Intensive. She premiered her solo show *White Man's Indian* at Summerworks 2017 in Toronto, where she was awarded the Emerging Artist Award. *The War Being Waged*, produced by Winnipeg's Prairie Theatre Exchange, has been acknowledged by Toronto critic Lynn Slotkin with a Tootsie Award.

Acknowledgements

I would like to acknowledge all of the incredible artists who brought their artistic excellence to the production of *The War Being Waged*, along with the backstage team that were able to carry seamlessly all that this show needs.

Andy Moro
MJ Dandeneau
Jera Wolfe
Brenda McLean
Tracey Nepinak
Emily Solstice Tait
Tantoo Cardinal
Karyn Kumhyr
Mike Duggan
Aileen Audette

And of course, Thomas Morgan Jones, who believed in this story from the very beginning.

Playwright's Note

The story you are about to experience is incredibly personal to me. It is based on one of my deepest fears, my experiences and as well is a response to one of the most important questions we ask ourselves as Indigenous people: What are you fighting for? In it you will find remnants of real people, real conflicts and real relationships. I hope you're ready to listen with an open heart.

Foreword

When asked, "What is *The War Being Waged* about?" Darla always answered, "It is about the question we ask ourselves as Indigenous people every day: What are we fighting for?"

Woman. Mother. Artist. Activist. Warrior. Poet. Philosopher.

Darla Contois.

Her journey of writing this profound text (in all the ways that text can mean in a performance context) has been extraordinary and quite unlike anything I have witnessed before.

It began with a telephone conversation in 2018. I asked Darla if she would like to write a play as a commission with Prairie Theatre Exchange (PTE). And on instinct, I asked if she would like to write for movement or dance. She lit up, explaining that she had always wanted to write for dance or movement, but was unsure how to begin. We agreed to begin together, her courageously entering into the unknown of story and form, and PTE supporting her.

The first writing that arrived was a series of poems under the title *LOVE*. When talking about these poems, she shared that they were about self-harm and suicide in her community. She believed that the only way through, the only way to find hope, and the only way to change, was love. And though she wasn't happy with the initial poetry, the potency of the words was astonishing.

There were several drafts of this poetry before Darla expressed that she was stuck with the writing. She didn't know which way to go. And then she was silent for a time. Months later, an email arrived with new writing. This time, the poems were gone. In their place was an early draft of a piece of prose for a solo voice, what would become Part One of *The War Being Waged*. I remember being breathless at the end of reading the draft. When I asked her what had inspired the change of direction, she said she didn't know. This new story had arrived, and so she followed her instincts. A whole new world of story had opened up, with new characters, and a new narrative. That said, it was clear that these pieces were connected. That they were speaking to the same world. From the same world.

Canada always wins.
They take everything.

And then, two major events occurred. There was a pandemic. And Darla became a mother.

In discussion with Darla, we realized that the short story was from the voice of a grandmother. And she now knew that she wanted to begin again with the poetry, to write from the voice of a mother. She had so much to say, so many new insights since the birth of her daughter. And we realized together, all these years later, that the final piece of the story was for a granddaughter. And that it would all be in dance. That Darla, three years later, would write her dance.

And there it was. A story across three generations of Indigenous women. A story, and a performance text, that spanned three performance genres.

Of necessity, we knew that to realize the play, Darla would have to write alongside other collaborators. And so, the production team came together. Each of them read Part One, and were told the story of what Part Two and Three would eventually become. Without question, without hesitation, each of them said yes. They all took a leap of faith. They all believed in Darla, her story, and the potential of what this project could be.

We met regularly over the course of a year leading to production. Designer, composer, and choreographer also worked on commission to create alongside Darla. The meetings were non-hierarchical, with every artist sharing and contributing to each other's discipline. Designers discussing writing, composer shaping image, choreographers shaping music, and so on. When it came time to create the video content, Darla wrote design prompts in poetry as she had written dance through words. And we all swam through that language together, looking for inspirations, clues, clarity, and more questions. And through these meetings, always with a focus on Darla's writing and story, the set emerged. A 30-minute video of design research emerged. The voice recordings emerged. The full composition of music for Parts Two and Three emerged. And the choreography, through the choreographer and dancer, took shape.

Darla invited Andy, Emily, Jera, MJ, Tantoo, and Tracey to have a kind of authorship in the telling of the story. She trusted them to create with her and also apart from her. To inform and inspire her, and to challenge her. She fully embraced an approach whereby every element of production was, in its own way, text. And she celebrated these artists by letting them dream. And play. With open hearts.

I opened my eyes
and
I saw light
joy
wonder

We all watched in awe as Darla navigated the process.

We let her teach us through the wisdom of her words.

Through her vulnerability.

Through her truths.

And we saw the cost. The toll it took on her.

It cost everyone on the production.

But it gave so much more.

To each artist.

nitanis
we are all connected

For a play that speaks to so much injustice and turmoil, it is a play about hope.

It is a play that celebrates beauty.

A play that finds the potential for beauty, everywhere.

Deep Breath

Four years after she set the first words down, while none of the original poems of LOVE remain, I am continuously reminded that this had all begun as a play about love. Darla's initial instinct was love. That the way through, the way forward, was love.

The play answers the question, "What are we fighting for?" in many different ways. And it invites the audience to find their own answers. But as we all witnessed the audience meet this work for the first time, and then as we watched hearts and minds meet it again and again over 20 performances, it was clear that LOVE was an answer to the question.

*The only thing that makes sense to me
is home*

—Thomas Morgan Jones
Treaty 1 Territory, Winnipeg, 2022

Thomas Morgan Jones is the artistic director of Prairie Theatre Exchange.

Production History

The War Being Waged was commissioned by Prairie Theatre Exchange and first produced by PTE as part of their 2021/22 season under the artistic direction of Thomas Morgan Jones. Run dates were November 3–21, 2021.

Cast

Tracey Nepinak

Emily Solstice Tait

Voice of Tantoo Cardinal

Creative Team

Director: .... Thomas Morgan Jones

Associate Director: .... Darla Contois

Set/Lighting/Projection Design: .... Andy Moro

Costume Design: .... Andy Moro with Brenda McLean

Composer/Sound Design: .... MJ Dandeneau

Choreographer: ....Jera Wolfe

Stage Manager: ....Karyn Kumhyr

Assistant Stage Manager: ....Mike Duggan

Make-up: .... Andy Moro with Aileen Audette

Production Notes

This is a play with two performers, an older female actor and a young female dancer. However, it is a story of three generations of women, an Indigenous family from Canada told through interdisciplinary ways of storytelling.

Part One follows the grandmother, as she retells the story of her life and how she came to be in prison; this fact should not become apparent to the audience until she reveals it. **Part Two** is a representation from the perspective of the mother, told through spoken word poetry as well as visual representations on stage, using the motif of each poem with your performers. Feel free to add music, projections, and anything else you feel helps you to flesh out the life of each poem. **Part Three** is the story of the granddaughter, told through dance. The prompts you see represent the journey the dancer should follow with movement.

Any stage directions included in this version of the script represent how the story was told on stage at the Prairie Theatre Exchange world premiere in 2021.

Tracey Nepinak in the 2021 Prairie Theatre Exchange world premiere.
Photo by Joey Senft.

Tracey Nepinak and Emily Solstice Tait in the 2021 Prairie Theatre
Exchange world premiere. Photo by Joey Senft.

Tracey Nepinak and Emily Solstice Tait in the 2021 Prairie Theatre
Exchange world premiere. Photo by Joey Senft.

Tracey Nepinak and Emily Solstice Tait in the 2021 Prairie Theatre
Exchange world premiere. Photo by Joey Senft.

Tracey Nepinak and Emily Solstice Tait in the 2021 Prairie Theatre Exchange world premiere. Photo by Joey Senft.

Tracey Nepinak in the 2021 Prairie Theatre Exchange world premiere. Photo by Joey Senft.

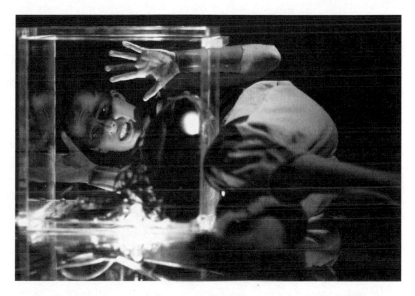

Emily Solstice Tait in the 2021 Prairie Theatre Exchange world premiere. Photo by Joey Senft.

Tracey Nepinak and Emily Solstice Tait in the 2021 Prairie Theatre Exchange world premiere. Photo by Joey Senft.

Tracey Nepinak and Emily Solstice Tait in the 2021 Prairie Theatre Exchange world premiere. Photo by Joey Senft.

Part One

Sometime in the not-so-distant future.

A GRANDMOTHER (60s) enters from stage right. She is wearing a grey shawl over what appears to be a very basic outfit. Almost unidentifiable. She moves slowly. She sits on a clear box centre stage surrounded by clear walls. She is well lit.

Throughout this monologue she plays with her hands—ever so gently. She fiddles with the ribbons from the shawl. She shows very little emotion—as if it's too unbearable to let it out.

She is beautiful, and you can imagine what she looked like as a younger adult. She is soft-spoken—but very direct and strong.

The GRANDMOTHER speaks.

I didn't know you were coming.

Beat.

I'm sorry.

Beat.

I'm going to tell you the truth.

I was born in Winnipeg, Manitoba and so were my older brothers. Although we were raised on Treaty 5 territory on the reserve. I didn't know my dad. We were raised on the shores where the Saskatchewan River meets Lake Winnipeg, the greatest body of water in all of Manitoba.
Kisiskatchewani Sipi, the rapid flowing river.
Hearing the waves crash and the trees blowing in the wind was the music of my childhood.
This was my home.
Our home for many generations.

My big brother had a problem with me my entire life. I don't know why. I suspected it was because Mum had always wanted a girl and he was first-born. He was disgusted with my presence and bullied me to the point of nearly breaking my wrist one summer. We were playing "blackout." The rules go that you choke one person until they pass out and when they wake up they chase you around the neighbourhood. My big brother was "it," and I remember when he woke up he chased after only me. Everyone else ran so fast I couldn't keep track of where they were all hiding. Next thing you know he was grabbing a huge log and hitting me in the gut as hard as he could. I fell down and he grabbed my arm and started twisting my wrist further and further when my younger brother showed up. The younger of the two anyhow, he was still older than me. He fought big brother off and brought me inside. He put ice on my wrist and said, "You'll be okay, just breathe."
I never tried to play with my big brother ever again.

I remember my youngest brother was always looking out for me and making sure that I didn't feel left out. He became my protector.

As we got older things got harder; especially after my grandma and grandpa died. One right after the other. It was like before you finished crying, the next one was already gone. I don't think Mum could handle it so she left and went back to university. We were left to fend for ourselves. She put my big brother in charge. He was very strict with me. I hated it.

My protector grew apart from me when he found his girlfriend. She used to come over a lot. They liked to be alone together. My big brother still hated the sight of me and I didn't have anyone else to talk to. I wasn't very good at making friends.
So I tried to kill myself.
I was a very dramatic teenager.
I remember my protector walking in on me in the bathroom.
It was the only time I'd ever seen him scared.

> *Beat.*

He cleaned me up and he never mentioned it again, not even to me. I was thankful for that. I was so ashamed.
I am my mum's only daughter.

Next thing his girlfriend got pregnant. It was a huge scandal on our reserve because they were only seventeen and her family were outsiders. They were white. Her parents were carefully polite and racist. They didn't think my brother was good enough for her. So he joined the army.
He was gone for months at a time training all over Canada.
Mum said, "He's the pride of our family."

The next few years flew by, my protector was home on and off—we stopped having things to talk about.

After I graduated high school I wanted to leave the reserve. I had dreams of an education. I'd been working as a waitress saving up my money.
I was finally ready to go when I learned I was pregnant.

My ex didn't care—our breakup was stone-cold nasty.
So I left anyway—went all the way to Toronto.

I had to raise my little girl alone and go to school.
It was hard.
We spent a lot of time in class talking about injustice.

There was so much interconnected—you know—the media, policies, political parties and ughh... it was so infuriating learning that our population had become so small and divided. I started to see why our lives were so unfair. Why Grandma and Grandpa hadn't received proper healthcare, why my dad wasn't able to be there for me because of his trauma in residential schools, why my language and culture were stolen from me, why I was made to feel like I don't belong here. It all became so clear and, even worse, it was all entirely true.

Beat.

The truth broke my heart.

When I graduated I was a different person. I wasn't interested in being a "Good Indian." I wanted out of the Indian Act. I wanted to change the future for my family, for my baby, to help out in any way that I could.

Beat.

But I wasn't sure how to do that.

Beat.

I moved back to Manitoba so baby could start school—be closer to my family. My big brother had been watching the house on the reserve—playing his guitar in the local bar. I tried to talk to him about what I'd learned but he didn't want to hear it. He wasn't interested in "politics." My protector was doing nothing but working, drinking and sleeping. Him and his girlfriend had gotten married while I was away. My nephew had grown up. They had another baby on the way. When I got back, for a while it was like things could go back to normal between us—but we could only talk when we were drinking together.
It was painful.
He was different too. Everything in his mind was a competition. He was constantly shining his shoes and ironing his clothes because he was told he had to be an "upstanding citizen." He was obsessed with being the best—with getting promoted. He was praised by his commanding officers and they really liked the way he was mentoring young Native soldiers—taking initiative. Mum was really proud of him.

I hated everything the army stood for and how they protected Canada's interests, but I couldn't tell my family that. Ipperwash, Oka, and residential schools. They tore our nations apart. My protector believed in taking orders and that's the same mentality that slaughtered us—that continues the genocide of our people.

They're just doing their job.

It was hard for me to be around him—to have my baby girl around him.

But Mum always taught me that family is the most important thing.

He decided to take care of his family using the army as a security blanket and it led us on two very different sides of...

Silence.

Still—he's my brother.

My protector.

I have so many great memories from when we were kids on the reserve.

He was promoted and stationed in Ottawa.

He took his family and they moved.

It was a relief—I was tired of pretending.

I was glad to stay in Winnipeg with Mum. But things got worse living in the city—Indigenous women and girls started to go missing, one right after the other. "Domestic violence, drugs, life on the street." It was like the news couldn't understand they were our daughters. It was our fault. The worst was when a young girl went missing and was found wrapped up in a blanket in the Red River.

She was fourteen years old.

Her murderer was found not guilty.

Tina Fontaine.

I cried the night the verdict was announced. I did something I'd never done before. I set up a tent outside the Manitoba legislative building. I camped for eleven days in the middle of winter. Mum thought I was crazy, she didn't like that I left my baby girl at home, but I knew she was well taken care of. It was exhilarating; I was doing something real, instead of sitting at home waiting for things to change on their own. I had people join me—people send support from all over the country. Camps with my spirit name went up in Regina, Calgary and Toronto. I wasn't sure what I'd started but it felt good to be taking control.

In the end it was all for nothing. Governments don't care about demonstrations, they don't care how much noise you make. The policies can only be changed one way; the government way.
To them, we don't matter.
It's better if we're gone.

That was a hard pill to swallow—but I was glad that at least I found my kind of people. My new friends introduced me to "Sovereignty," they called it. We wanted to be safe and take care of our own. We wanted to stop being exploited and lied to. We wanted what our original ancestors agreed to in those treaties. They introduced me to the legal rights we hold as Indigenous people and how it is our duty to protect all that we hold sacred.

This was the first time I felt my place in the world actually made sense.

This was the first time I could see a safe future for my baby girl.

We spent years working together building a grassroots organization. We fed the homeless, put together demonstrations, and even printed our own magazines.

Being a part of a community for the first time in my life changed everything. This was where I belonged. My baby girl was doing well in school, we were all happy. Mum said she was proud of me and that I was doing work that was going to truly make a difference. Which was confusing because she said the same thing to my brother.

I was watching the news. A Native fisherman had caught a two-headed fish in Lake Winnipeg and people were baffled by it.
This wasn't the first time it's happened.
The city along with Hydro have been dumping who knows what into the lake for years unnoticed.

It wasn't hard for us to agree to focus on the health of the lake. As a starting point we publicly demanded that the City of Winnipeg stop dumping chemicals and sewage into the lake. We printed a public letter—went to social media—did interviews.

Our organization started getting messages from people that for years had been documenting how the fish were declining—weird deformities in the plant and animal life. Things they'd never seen or even smelled before. They sent us videos, letters, pictures, and even their melted boots.
The City of Winnipeg's water treatment plant was still ignoring us when we started our demonstration on their front step. The amount of information we had was disturbing.

Within a week the reserves up north were joining us. They created barricades to prevent traffic from travelling through their communities.
Semi-trucks with goods travelling important Manitoba highways were getting backed up. In the news, companies were angry the money was slowing down.
The city sent in officials to negotiate we vacate with a promise they would have a plan in sixty days to solve the problem.
We refused.
We wanted it all to stop immediately.
The city said the health of its residents would be at risk—backed-up sewage with nowhere to go.

A week went by with no movement by the city, our camp or the barricades. That's when Winnipeggers signed petitions that the city plow down our camp without notice. They started a protest outside city hall.

Winnipeg police started making arrests at our camp.

Our supporters at the barricades started welcoming the settler communities along the shorelines to join us.

That was a turning point.

We all wanted the same thing: clean, safe water.

Mum wanted me to come home—she was tired of babysitting. She said I had a choice to make, either I come home or she wasn't coming by the camp anymore with my baby—"It's getting too dangerous." We got into a big fight.

How could she not see how important this was?

Beat.

I had to stay.

RCMP began shooting tear gas, sending in dogs and using rubber bullets to disperse the barricades up north but none of it was working. The more violent they became, the more people joined our side. Solidarity groups popped up all across the country.

The hydro dams were shut down—no workers could get through.

Beat.

That's when the City of Winnipeg called in the Armed Forces. Eight weeks and now we were facing off with 500 Canadian soldiers.

We created a perimeter to keep them at least 100 metres from the camp.

Beat.

We are free to our self-determination anywhere on our own land. It's the law.
This is treaty territory.

Myself and three others were on the frontlines.

It was midday shift and I hadn't slept more than five hours in the past three days. 11:37 a.m. I'll never forget it.

I was holding the handgun I'd been given to protect myself— looking out at the soldiers when one started coming toward me. He was holding his arms up, rifle in hand, and as he got closer my stomach started to sink. I started to sweat. I couldn't breathe good—my face was covered. The soldier's face grew familiar with every step he took and I was frozen. It was my brother. My protector. He was wearing a helmet but I recognized his eyes and his dark skin. All the other soldiers were white.

In the army you're allowed to remove yourself from situations involving your own people. It's a safety net for Indigenous soldiers. My brother told me that.

Beat.

How could he be here?

He stood in front of me just staring—I could feel the hardness in his body. The trained movements. He'd been instructed to let us know the standoff had gone on long enough. He and his men were given orders to move us aside, "no questions asked," five minutes ago.

I was still.
I didn't know what to do.
I could hear my breath shaking.

When I heard his voice, it broke me—I went to hand him my gun.
I must've done something wrong because he mistook my surrender for resistance.

He grabbed the gun so quick and my glove was caught behind the trigger.
I tried to untangle myself—but my gun went off.
I told them not to load my gun!
I fell to the ground.
He fell in front of me.
There was blood everywhere.

The next time I opened my eyes I was in an ambulance.
I was in handcuffs.

I wanted my baby.

I was shot in the shoulder by another soldier. I thought I was going to die. Staring up at those lights in that ambulance—I didn't care anymore. I wanted to take it all back. I didn't want to fight anymore.

There was this fishing trip we'd taken at the lake when I was small. My protector taught me how to use a fishing rod.
I fell asleep waiting for him and he carried me home.
I wanted to take your mum fishing there like my brother did for me.

When we got to the hospital I remember the officers telling the doctor I was dangerous.

(She mocks an officer.) "This one's a savage."

After surgery the police questioned me from my hospital bed.
I was handcuffed 24/7 with an armed guard outside my room.

That's when they told me I'd killed that soldier.
I killed my brother.

I asked the officers if they could notify my family. They said they did. I waited for my mum to visit but she never came. The only person I saw was a CFS worker. She came in and said that if I didn't give Mum custody of my baby girl she would end up in foster care.
I had no choice.

I was the Indian who killed a soldier. A True Canadian Soldier who was only protecting his country from terrorists.

I was heartless when the media learned that he was my brother.

My trial was expedited, front page news for weeks. When I was brought into the court room I saw my brother's wife. She never looked at me. Mum wasn't there.

Life without parole.
I never thought I'd ever see anyone from my family ever again.
I have a granddaughter.

> THE GRANDDAUGHTER enters from stage left. She walks slowly to her place behind the GRANDMOTHER. She is dressed in an outfit that resembles a warrior. She has a painted face—but she is still so young. A teenager.

Lillian. You are so beautiful.
That was my mum's name.

Canada always wins.
They take everything.

If you can ever forgive me then please tell your mum I'm sorry.

Part Two

Scene 1

Music begins—a deep bass tone—into a slow drum and a heartbeat.

The GRANDMOTHER stands—takes the shawl from her back, folds it up nicely and places it inside the box she has been sitting on.

The world we are in is dark—filled with sharp lighting along the clear walls of the world.

Through this movement of the GRANDMOTHER—we hear this first poem in a voiceover.

The GRANDMOTHER's outfit is revealed to have prison logos on it under her shawl.

The beating of the drum
never stops
it is
only
handed down
from
generation to generation
heartbeat after heartbeat
we are all one

Scene 2

THE GRANDMOTHER comes to look at her GRANDDAUGHTER through the clear glass wall. They share a glance before the grandmother exits.

The GRANDDAUGHTER encloses the world a bit more—shifting the clear walls into herself.

She is now alone—standing on the box. Feeling and representing herself being trapped in her movements.

The lighting is stark and dramatic. As this is happening, canvas see-through projection walls are being lowered in front of her.

She pushes out the walls—with great effort—as we hear this next poem in a voiceover.

Anything
that

reminds
reminds
reminds

me

of

my

mother

Scene 3

We begin to see projections of colour around her, as the sound design shifts to a slow piano. She moves around the stage—feeling lost. The GRANDMOTHER re-enters with the same images and gestures in her body as the GRANDDAUGHTER did when she first entered. The GRANDMOTHER is now in a long skirt—warrior-like.

They are now in a new world together— existing but not quite interacting with each other—looking around to discover.

The GRANDMOTHER sees the GRANDDAUGHTER and begins to mimic her childlike movements, slowly. They move around in unison—the GRANDMOTHER witnessing the GRANDDAUGHTER.

The GRANDDAUGHTER finally sees her—and they meet centre stage, hovering over the shawl encased in the clear box between them.

They see it and sit back to back on the box and sway as we hear this next poem in voiceover.

A gentle nod in the music to "You Are My Sunshine."

I remember
the gentle
the soft
the all knowing
voice

Singing me to sleep

You are my sunshine

Scene 4

*GRANDMOTHER and GRAND-
DAUGHTER come apart as the music
enters a new phase—faster and more
playful. The projections surrounding them
take us into a new world—filled with balls
of light—feeling wonderous.*

*GRANDMOTHER gets up abruptly—as
GRANDDAUGHTER shifts her body to
her every move, watching curiously.*

*As GRANDDAUGHTER is still sitting
on the clear box centre stage, she crosses her
legs. GRANDMOTHER comes to stand
behind her as we hear this next poem in
voiceover.*

My greatest gift
My blood is yours
and we are tied together
Forever

My baby girl

I will protect you
and
you will know *love*

Scene 5

We hear a howling wind in the sound design. The GRANDDAUGHTER comes to move with the sound of the wind—into standing on top of the clear box centre stage. She attempts to grasp at the wind—unable to catch it.

As GRANDMOTHER sits in front of her. A crackling of fire and we see the projections shift to a fiery orange tone. We hear a rattle settle slowly into the world around us.

As this next poem is read in voiceover.

Sit still
Listen
Hear
The wind knows how to whisper only
through the trees
Water falls upon the shore like coming
home only to leave again
Give
And
Take
Balance
Neither
Here

Nor

There
Unseen
Nowhere
And yet
Everywhere
The earth will hold you
Sing to you
Breathe to you
And *love* you

Forever

Scene 6

We can see water faintly in the world around us—through projection. The GRANDDAUGHTER comes down and meets the GRANDMOTHER on the ground. GRANDMOTHER leans back into the warmth and safety of GRANDDAUGHTER's hands. The music is beautiful with a soft piano melody.

The GRANDDAUGHTER suddenly moves away from her GRAND-MOTHER—quickly and playfully, she dances across the stage as we hear this next poem in voiceover. The GRAND-MOTHER watches.

The heart

is

an

imagination

to fool you into

believing

that **love**

comes from only one place

Scene 7

*The lighting goes dark as the GRAND-
MOTHER moves to the back of the stage,
not noticing the GRANDDAUGHTER
as she appears to be praying to the sky.
The GRANDDAUGHTER mimics her
movement as they open up the sky. The
projections are green—taking us again into
a new world.*

As we hear this next poem in voiceover.

Like the trees communicate
Deep
Beneath the surface
we
love
Deep
Beneath the surface

Scene 8

GRANDMOTHER and GRAND-
DAUGHTER acknowledge each other and
reach out towards one another—unable
to make a connection before the GRAND-
MOTHER steps away. She is approached
again by the GRANDDAUGHTER but
moves away. They both acknowledge the
distance between them—separated by the
shawl encased in the box centre stage.

As we hear this next poem in voiceover.

I opened my eyes
and
I saw light
joy
wonder
everything that I remember
when I was
a kid
who was told
I didn't know anything
and yet
my eyes were
the only ones that were
open

Scene 9

The GRANDMOTHER comes to stand on the clear box centre stage—as the GRANDDAUGHTER falls to the ground. GRANDMOTHER acknowledges the sky—as we hear a faint singing from ancestors in the sound design. The GRANDMOTHER appears to be falling off—as the GRANDDAUGHTER comes to catch her. She pulls away as they are yet again separated by the shawl between them. GRANDMOTHER lies on the ground— as the GRANDDAUGHTER shifts her body into quick agile movements, cradling herself throughout her movements around the stage.

We hear a rattle—the music is still slow.

The next poem is read in Cree—as we see the GRANDMOTHER and the GRANDDAUGHTER come to a standing position separated by the clear box centre stage.

In the projections, a spirit appears between them as they mimic the movement of each other. A big giant deep breath—in all four directions.

The spirit turns to smoke.

Her absence
shattered

everything

and that's all I remember
about the love we had

Scene 10

GRANDMOTHER and GRAND-
DAUGHTER are moving around the
stage—slowly—gesturing and alluding
to smudging. As this next poem is read in
voiceover.

We can hear a drum and we can see fire,
smoke, grass and light all around us. The
crackling of a fire. We see the spirit—in
smoke—again.

The first time I smelled
the burning sage
the sweetgrass
the tobacco
the cedar

I knew

Generations
of
love
had been sent
to protect me

Scene 11

A rhythmic beat comes in—as the GRANDDAUGHTER gets faster and more abrupt in her movements. The GRANDMOTHER begins to mimic her— but only as far as her body will allow. The music gets louder—faster—and comes to a silence.

As we hear this next poem in voiceover.

How can I ever feel alone again
after
giving birth
and experiencing the **greatest pain**
I will ever know that

generations of mothers

have gladly gone through
and only through
to get here
to me
and
to you

nitanis
we are all connected

Scene 12

The GRANDDAUGHTER comes to the ground slowly as GRANDMOTHER watches. A beautiful piano melody enters the sound design as GRANDMOTHER reaches for the GRANDDAUGHTER. A slow wave on the shore in the sound design—as she gets closer and closer to nearly making a connection. She pulls away and turns away just before they do. As the GRANDDAUGHTER reaches for her.

We hear this next poem in voiceover.

she

prayed for
wished for
dreamed for

me

and here I am

the
only daughter
of an
only daughter

Scene 13

GRANDMOTHER exits.

The GRANDDAUGHTER comes to use the clear box with the shawl to bring herself back up to standing. She is visibly struggling on the ground — using all of her might. A strong drumbeat enters the sound design as she makes her way up to sitting on the box.

As we hear this next poem in voiceover.

they say
love hurts
not understanding
that love is the
only
thing
that will *never*

Part Three

The GRANDDAUGHTER is now sitting on the clear box encasing the shawl — she looks tired and worn-out. Her expression is troubled as we come into the final movement piece of the play. Her journey is of being isolated and separated from her family — into the feeling of acceptance.

It is not an easy journey. It is represented through these movement prompts:

1.

It feels impossible to move without making the wrong choice. It feels hopeless to even try. My blood will forever belong to the warriors that fought to get me here. Was I worth it? I'm too scared to make a mistake. Either way, it feels like a losing battle.

Help me.

I need to breathe.
I need to be strong even when I feel like I'm falling apart.

2.

Like fear so bad you shake
Can't sleep
Can't eat
Paralyzing Fear

3.

Deep Breath

4.

The woods and water are safe
Home is safe
Take me home
To where I am free and allowed to be me
I can love and give and be a part of the community
The only thing that makes sense to me
is home

The War Being Waged Study Guide

Discussion Questions:

1. What does the title of the play mean to you?

2. What is your knowledge of Indigenous peoples in Canada? Do you think that your idea of Indigenous peoples has been shaped by media stereotypes?

3. How do you think this play relates to real life? Do you think it does at all?

4. What is the role of the arts in your life?

5. How important is an open mind when you begin to read or listen to a story? How does having an open mind affect your experience?

6. Did you learn or hear anything new from reading this play?

7. What responsibility, if any, do you carry after reading the play?

8. In *The War Being Waged*, our main character discusses being painted as a villain in the media. How do you think media representations affect Indigenous people?

9. What role did the law play in the outcome of this story?

10. Do you think that the grandmother did the right thing? What would you have done?

11. How do you think culture and tradition affect Indigenous people who are dealing with trauma?

12. Did your opinion or understanding of the Canadian/ Indigenous peoples relationship change after reading this book?

Colonial Practices and Policies

Canadian colonial practices and policies such as the *Indian Act*, the pass system, reserves, and residential schools sought to control and assimilate Indigenous peoples. These practices and policies have had severe historic and ongoing impacts on generations of Indigenous peoples.

The following subjects are addressed or alluded to in *The War Being Waged:*

Indigenous Incarceration Rates

Indigenous incarceration rates are at an all-time high, according to reports made in December 2021 by Canada's correctional investigator. Dr. Ivan Zinger predicts that with this trajectory, Canada will reach "historic and unconscionable levels" of Indigenous incarceration in federal penitentiaries.

A Justice Canada study has found that its own criminal courts are stacked against Indigenous defendants: Indigenous people were found to be 33% less likely to be acquitted, and 14% more likely to plead or be found guilty. Once convicted, Indigenous offenders were 30% more likely to be imprisoned.

First Nations, Inuit and Métis women and girls are overrepresented in Canada's criminal justice system as both victims and survivors. Indigenous women make up 48% of the total population of women in correctional facilities within Canada, yet they make up less than 5% of the total population of people in Canada. A substantial body of research points to gendered impacts of colonialism as a central factor in the under-protection and over-criminalization of Indigenous women and girls.

The Justice Canada study concluded the criminal courts are "contributing to differential and disproportionate outcomes for Indigenous people." This represents clear evidence of systemic injustice.

Learn more: Research the cases of Connie Oakes, Donald Marshall Jr., Tammy Marquardt, Wilson Nepoose, William Mullins-Johnson, and Maxwell and Tori-Anne Johnson.

The *Indian Act*

The *Indian Act* is legislation that was enacted in 1876 and still remains as Canadian law. It consolidated a number of earlier colonial laws that sought to control and assimilate Indigenous peoples into white Christian culture, and has been amended many times over the years to do away with some of its more egregiously restrictive and oppressive laws. However, the *Act* has had historic and ongoing impacts on First Nations cultures, economies, politics and communities. It has also caused inter-generational trauma, particularly with regards to residential schools.

Among other things, the *Indian Act* gave the government control of Indigenous elections on reserves; it forced Indigenous children to attend residential schools, and it gave the ownership of land to treaty bands. It also prevented Indigenous people from practising their culture, legislated who women were allowed to marry (if they wanted to keep their status,) and even affected whether or not Indigenous people could possess and enact a last will and testament.

Many have called for the *Indian Act* to be abolished. However, the *Indian Act* legally distinguishes between First Nations and other Canadians, and it acknowledges that the federal government has a unique relationship with, and obligation to, First Nations. For this reason, the idea of the abolition of the *Indian Act* has been controversial. Although there are many differing opinions on how to confront the issues presented by the *Indian Act*, leaders widely agree that if any alternative political relationship is to be worked out between First Nations and the government, First Nations will need to be active participants in establishing it.

Learn more: *Listen to* The Secret Life of Canada *podcast S2 episode "The Indian Act."* https://www.cbc.ca/radio/secretlifeofcanada/what-do-you-really-know-about-the-indian-act-1.5188255

Self-Determination and the Doctrine of Discovery

In *The War Being Waged*, the grandmother character addresses the subject of self-determination. Self-determination refers to the right of a people to freely determine their own political status, take control of their economic, social, and cultural development, and to have the ability to benefit from and dispose of their inherent natural resources as they see fit. Officially, the Government of Canada recognizes the right of Indigenous peoples to self-determination, as it is obligated to do under international treaty law. Yet in recent years we have seen many Indigenous communities rising up to protest incursions on their territories, only to be met with extreme force from RCMP and the military.

UNB law professor Benjamin Perryman wrote, with regard to the Wet'suwet'en pipeline protests: "According to the Supreme Court of Canada, Indigenous people may hold 'Aboriginal title' to their traditional territory but only in relation to the Crown's sovereignty. The Crown was able to assert this sovereignty because hundreds of years ago the land was considered 'empty' by Europeans and therefore available to be 'discovered' by Europeans. This 'doctrine of discovery' has never been renounced by Canadian courts nor have courts explained how its inherent racism can be justified in a modern constitutional democracy...If the rule of law is premised on the notion that we are all equal before law, Canadian courts must be able to explain why Wet'suwet'en law that predates the Canadian constitution is irrelevant...If that explanation rests on the 'doctrine of discovery,' courts must be able to explain why that ongoing reliance is justified. In the absence of such justifications, we will be able to dispossess Indigenous people from their land by force under cover of law, but we will be unable to plausibly claim that our constitutional order rests on a rule of law principle worthy of respect. If left untreated, the ongoing oppression of Indigenous people in Canada risks causing an irreparable blight on our constitutional order." (*Toronto Star*, November 29, 2021.)

Learn more: *Read the United Nations Declaration of Indigenous Rights.*

Residential Schools

In *The War Being Waged*, the main character mentions residential schools and how they affected her life. These were schools that Indigenous children were forced to attend and live in, government-sponsored schools that were run by Christian churches. Their purpose was to isolate Indigenous children from their families, culture, language, and communities, instead teaching them religion, Canadian culture, and the English language in order to encourage assimilation into white society. These schools existed from 1870 to 1996. The attempts to assimilate Indigenous children began as soon as they arrived at the school; boys' long hair was cut short, and the children were given uniforms (and often new names.) The curriculum focused on Christian practices and denigrated Indigenous spiritual traditions. In its Final Report, the Truth and Reconciliation Commission of Canada called the Indian residential school system "cultural genocide."

Over 150,000 children attended these schools, and the system disrupted Indigenous practices, culture, and language, preventing them from being taught to younger generations. John Tootoosis, a former residential school student, says of a child who has been through the residential school system, "On one side are all the things he learned from his people and their way of life that was being wiped out, and on the other side are the white man's ways which he could never fully understand since he never had the right amount of education and could not be part of it. There he is, hanging in the middle of two cultures and he is not a white man and he is not an Indian. They washed away practically everything from our minds, all the things an Indian needed to help himself, to think the way a human person should in order to survive." *(Canadian Encyclopedia)*

The Canadian government didn't properly document or care how children were being treated in these schools, and often, priests and nuns and other clergy had complete power over the children. Beatings, starvation, isolation, medical experimentation, and many other horrific things happened to these children while they were under the care of these people. The emotional, mental, and physical abuse suffered at residential schools still affects Indigenous families today. Children who were abused in the schools sometimes went on to abuse others. Some developed addictions as a way of coping, and countless lives were lost to alcohol and drugs; families were destroyed.

Today, across the country, in places where these schools existed—in towns, reserves and cities—people are finding the unmarked graves of children who attended residential schools. These are children who never returned home to their families, and often no explanation was given as to how or why these children died. Indigenous people are working to recover these children and give them the peace and recognition they deserve.

Learn more: Read They Came for the Children *and the 94 Calls to Action of the Truth and Reconciliation Commission. Watch Tim Wolochatiuk's film,* We Were Children *and* Indian Horse, *based on the book by Richard Wagamese.*

Note: If you have been affected by the residential school system and need help, you can contact the 24-hour Indian Residential Schools Crisis Line at 1-866-925-4419.

The "Sixties Scoop" and the Child Welfare System

Despite having distinct linguistic, cultural, and political systems, many Indigenous peoples share common beliefs such as the interdependence of all living things, and a strong sense of community. This is reflected in their way of parenting and educating children, and traditionally all members of the community (especially Elders) participate in raising children. This was at odds with the European way of child-rearing, which centred on family units. Residential schools removed Indigenous children from their communities for decades, and when the schools began closing, the state intervened via child welfare agencies.

In 1951, changes to the *Indian Act* allowed provincial laws to apply on reserves. Child welfare authorities began apprehending children on reserves, leading to what is known as the "Sixties Scoop," a period in the 1960s and 1970s when large numbers of First Nations, Metis, and Inuit children were apprehended and placed into foster care, in most cases without the consent of their families or bands. On some reserves, nearly all newborn babies were taken from their mothers, and by the mid-70s, approximately 70% of children in foster care were First Nations, Metis, or Inuit. In most cases, the children of the "Sixties Scoop" were placed into the homes of Euro-Canadian families. (As well, large numbers of children were sent to white families in the USA.) This resulted in tremendous obstacles to the development of a healthy identity for many children, who were not able to learn their languages or traditions, or sometimes even to know their backgrounds.

During the 1980s, the government made changes that allowed Indigenous child welfare services to operate, but sadly, problems persist. In 2021, more than half of all children in foster care are Indigenous, although they only represent 7.7% of Canada's child population. The attempts to colonize and assimilate Indigenous people (such as residential schools and the Sixties Scoop) have resulted in intergenerational trauma that continues to destroy Indigenous families.

Learn more: Watch this interview with Pam Palmater, who discusses the child welfare system with TVO's Steve Paikin. https://www.youtube.com/watch?v=Wo713fVj9c4. *Read the play* In Care *by Kenneth T. Williams.*

Media Stereotypes

For too long, white settler society has controlled the way that Indigenous people are portrayed in the media. In the news, reporters often fall back on stereotypes: Indigenous people in general are often seen as resistant to progress, unintelligent, destructive, and stuck in the past. Stereotypes of Indigenous women are particularly pernicious: they are often portrayed as drunks or addicts, as poor mothers, or as having an "at-risk" lifestyle that can lead to death or disappearance. In films and television shows, Indigenous people are also stereotyped. They may be seen as childlike or simplistic, or, conversely, as mystical figures who dispense wisdom to white characters. The general public's opinion is informed by the news and the ways Indigenous people are portrayed in entertainment, and these stereotypes are both demeaning and destructive.

It's important to think objectively about the information you take in. Where does the news you consume come from? Who is reporting it? Who funded the creation of the film you're watching? Were any Indigenous people involved in its production? Too often in Canadian media we are not cognizant of the context of the media we are consuming.

Learn more: Watch films written and directed by Indigenous filmmakers. Read books by Indigenous authors. Watch APTN news reports and compare the reporting to the news programs you usually watch.

Protest

A protest is defined as a public expression of objection, the disapproval towards an idea or action that is typically political. A group of people come together to stand against what they feel is wrong, often ready to face the consequences that follow.

Indigenous people in recent years have protested about oil pipelines, mines, golf courses, burial grounds, etc, with the goal of protecting the land. This resistance is often seen as anti-progress and anti-economy and is constantly at odds with Canadians who seek to make more money and pay less tax, at any cost to the environment.

Protests by Indigenous people, no matter how peaceful, have almost always been met with force from police and the armed forces. Protesters have been given fines, been sentenced to jail time, have suffered injury and even death. All of this has led to further disenfranchisement from the inherent rights affirmed in the treaties.

The recent "freedom convoy" protests should make us question why such an aggressive gathering was allowed to continue for so long without experiencing the same brutality that Indigenous people have faced from the Canadian government.

The characters in *The War Being Waged* work to protect the land from harm. The grandmother character raises the question of being able to start a protest/demonstration on her own treaty territory and what that means when the relationship with Canada comes into question.

Learn more: *Research events such as the Oka Crisis, the Ipperwash Crisis, and the Gustafson Lake Stand-off to learn more about how Indigenous protesters have been treated in Canada.*

References

- *Toronto Star:* https://www.thestar.com/opinion/contributors/2021/11/29/rcmp-raids-on-indigenous-land-defenders-risk-causing-irreparable-damage-to-our-constitutional-order.html
- Government of Manitoba: https://www.edu.gov.mb.ca/k12/cur/socstud/foundation_gr6/blms/6-4-3d.pdf
- The Canadian Encyclopedia: https://www.thecanadianencyclopedia.ca/en/article/gustafsen-lake-standoff
- https://www.thecanadianencyclopedia.ca/en/article/oka-crisis
- https://www.thecanadianencyclopedia.ca/en/article/residential-schools
- https://www.thecanadianencyclopedia.ca/en/article/indian-act-plain-language-summary
- Carleton University: https://newsroom.carleton.ca/story/indigenous-black-protesters-treated-differently/
- Wikipedia: https://en.wikipedia.org/wiki/Influence_of_mass_media
- TV Ontario: https://www.tvo.org/article/rewriting-journalism-how-canadian-media-reinforces-indigenous-stereotypes
- Global News: https://globalnews.ca/news/8458351/canada-residential-schools-unmarked-graves-indigenous-impact/
- UBC: https://indigenousfoundations.arts.ubc.ca/the_indian_act/
- CBC: https://www.cbc.ca/radio/secretlifeofcanada/what-do-you-really-know-about-the-indian-act-1.5188255
- CBC: https://www.cbc.ca/news/politics/truth-and-reconciliation-94-calls-to-action-1.3362258

- TRC calls to action: https://publications.gc.ca/collections/collection_2015/trc/IR4-8-2015-eng.pdf

- They Came for the Children: https://publications.gc.ca/collections/collection_2012/cvrc-trcc/IR4-4-2012-eng.pdf

- United Nations: https://www.un.org/development/desa/indigenouspeoples/wp-content/uploads/sites/19/2018/11/UNDRIP_E_web.pdf

- Macleans: https://www.macleans.ca/news/canada/from-foster-care-to-missing-or-murdered-canadas-other-tragic-pipeline/

- TVO: https://www.youtube.com/watch?v=Wo7l3fVj9c4

- AFN: https://www.afn.ca/about-afn/declaration-of-first-nations/

A Declaration of First Nations:

We the Original Peoples of this land know
the Creator put us here.

The Creator gave us laws that govern all our relationships
to live in harmony with nature and mankind.

The Laws of the Creator defined our
rights and responsibilities.

The Creator gave us our spiritual beliefs, our languages,
our culture, and a place on Mother Earth which provided
us with all our needs.

We have maintained our Freedom, our Languages,
and our Traditions from time immemorial.

We continue to exercise the rights and fulfill the
responsibilities and obligations given to us by the Creator
for the land upon which we were placed.

The Creator has given us the right to govern ourselves
and the right to self- determination.

The rights and responsibilities given to us by the Creator
cannot be altered or taken away by any other Nation.

— *Assembly of First Nations*